EVERYDAY
BAKING

WARM & WONDERFUL FALL FLAVORS

Publications International, Ltd.

Photography on endsheets © Shutterstock.com.

Pictured on the front cover: Rustic Cranberry-Pear Galette *(page 94)*.

Pictured on the back cover *(clockwise from top)*: Orange Cinnamon Rolls *(page 14)*, Pumpkin Cheesecake Bars *(page 34)* and Glazed Applesauce Spice Cake *(page 72)*.

ISBN: 978-1-68022-467-2

Library of Congress Control Number: 2016934624

Manufactured in China.

8 7 6 5 4 3 2 1

Microwave Cooking: Microwave ovens vary in wattage. Use the cooking times as guidelines and check for doneness before adding more time.

TABLE OF CONTENTS

BREADS & MUFFINS

GINGERBREAD PEAR MUFFINS

1¾ cups all-purpose flour

⅓ cup sugar

2 teaspoons baking powder

¾ teaspoon ground ginger

¼ teaspoon baking soda

¼ teaspoon salt

¼ teaspoon ground cinnamon

⅓ cup milk

¼ cup vegetable oil

¼ cup light molasses

1 egg

1 medium pear, peeled and finely chopped

1. Preheat oven to 375°F. Line 12 standard (2½-inch) muffin cups with paper baking cups.

2. Sift flour, sugar, baking powder, ginger, baking soda, salt and cinnamon into large bowl.

3. Whisk milk, oil, molasses and egg in medium bowl until well blended. Stir in pear. Add to flour mixture; stir just until moistened. Spoon batter evenly into prepared muffin cups.

4. Bake 20 minutes or until toothpick inserted into centers comes out clean. Immediately remove from pan; cool on wire rack 10 minutes. Serve warm or cool completely.

BOSTON BLACK COFFEE BREAD

MAKES 10 TO 12 SERVINGS

½ cup rye flour

½ cup cornmeal

½ cup whole wheat flour

1 teaspoon baking soda

½ teaspoon salt

¾ cup strong brewed
   coffee, room
   temperature or cold

⅓ cup molasses

¼ cup canola oil

¾ cup raisins

1. Preheat oven to 325°F. Grease and flour 9×5-inch loaf pan.

2. Combine rye flour, cornmeal, whole wheat flour, baking soda and salt in large bowl; mix well.

3. Add coffee, molasses and oil; stir until mixture forms thick batter. Fold in raisins. Pour batter into prepared pan.

4. Bake 50 minutes or until toothpick inserted into center comes out clean. Cool completely in pan on wire rack.

TIP: To cool hot coffee quickly, pour it over 2 ice cubes in a measuring cup to measure ¾ cup total. Let stand 10 minutes to cool.

APPLE PIE MONKEY BREAD

MAKES ABOUT 12 SERVINGS

½ cup (1 stick) butter, divided

2 large apples (about 1 pound), peeled and cut into ½-inch pieces (Fuji, Granny Smith or Braeburn)

½ cup plus 1 tablespoon sugar, divided

2½ teaspoons ground cinnamon, divided

½ cup finely chopped pecans

2 packages (7½ ounces each) refrigerated buttermilk biscuits (10 biscuits per package)

1. Preheat oven to 350°F. Spray 9-inch deep-dish pie plate with nonstick cooking spray.

2. Melt ¼ cup butter in large skillet or saucepan over medium heat. Add apples, 1 tablespoon sugar and ½ teaspoon cinnamon; cook and stir 5 minutes or until apples are tender and glazed. Transfer to large bowl. Melt remaining ¼ cup butter in same skillet, stirring to scrape up any glaze. Cool slightly.

3. Combine pecans, remaining ½ cup sugar and 2 teaspoons cinnamon in medium bowl; mix well. Separate biscuits; cut each biscuit into 4 pieces with scissors. Dip biscuit pieces in melted butter; roll in pecan mixture to coat. Place one quarter of biscuit pieces in prepared pie plate; top with one quarter of apples. Repeat layers three times. Sprinkle with remaining pecan mixture; drizzle with remaining butter.

4. Bake 30 minutes or until biscuits are firm and topping is golden brown. Serve warm.

SWEET POTATO MUFFINS

MAKES 24 MUFFINS

2 cups all-purpose flour

¾ cup chopped walnuts

¾ cup golden raisins

½ cup packed brown sugar

1 tablespoon baking powder

1 teaspoon ground cinnamon

½ teaspoon salt

½ teaspoon baking soda

¼ teaspoon ground nutmeg

1 cup mashed cooked sweet potato

¾ cup milk

½ cup (1 stick) butter, melted

2 eggs, beaten

1½ teaspoons vanilla

1. Preheat oven to 400°F. Line 24 standard (2½-inch) muffin cups with paper baking cups or spray with nonstick cooking spray.

2. Combine flour, walnuts, raisins, brown sugar, baking powder, cinnamon, salt, baking soda and nutmeg in medium bowl; mix well.

3. Whisk sweet potato, milk, butter, eggs and vanilla in large bowl until well blended. Add flour mixture; stir just until moistened. Spoon batter evenly into prepared muffin cups.

4. Bake 15 minutes or until toothpick inserted into centers comes out clean. Cool in pans 5 minutes; remove to wire racks to cool completely.

ORANGE CINNAMON ROLLS

MAKES 18 ROLLS

½ cup packed brown sugar

3 tablespoons butter,
  melted, divided

1 tablespoon ground
  cinnamon

1 teaspoon grated
  orange peel

1 loaf (1 pound) frozen
  bread dough, thawed

⅓ cup raisins (optional)

½ cup powdered sugar,
  sifted

1 to 2 tablespoons
  orange juice

1. Grease 2 (8-inch) round cake pans. Combine brown sugar, 1 tablespoon butter, cinnamon and orange peel in small bowl; mix well.

2. Roll out dough into 18×8-inch rectangle on lightly floured surface. Brush dough with remaining 2 tablespoons butter; spread evenly with brown sugar mixture. Sprinkle with raisins, if desired.

3. Starting with long side, roll up dough jelly-roll style; pinch seam to seal. Cut crosswise into 1-inch slices; arrange slices cut sides up in prepared pans. Cover loosely with plastic wrap; let rise in warm place 30 to 40 minutes or until almost doubled in size. Preheat oven to 350°F.

4. Bake 18 minutes or until golden brown. Immediately remove to wire racks; cool slightly.

5. Whisk powdered sugar and orange juice in small bowl until smooth and consistency is thin enough to pour. Drizzle glaze over warm rolls.

APPLESAUCE-SPICE BREAD

MAKES 9 SERVINGS

1½ cups all-purpose flour

1 cup unsweetened applesauce

¾ cup packed brown sugar

¼ cup shortening

1 egg

1 teaspoon vanilla

¾ teaspoon baking soda

¾ teaspoon ground cinnamon

¼ teaspoon baking powder

¼ teaspoon salt

¼ teaspoon ground nutmeg

½ cup toasted chopped walnuts

½ cup raisins (optional)

Powdered sugar

1. Preheat oven to 350°F. Spray 9-inch square baking pan with nonstick cooking spray.

2. Beat flour, applesauce, brown sugar, shortening, egg, vanilla, baking soda, cinnamon, baking powder, salt and nutmeg in large bowl with electric mixer at low speed 30 seconds. Beat at high speed 3 minutes. Stir in walnuts and raisins, if desired. Pour batter into prepared pan.

3. Bake 30 minutes or until toothpick inserted into center comes out clean. Cool in pan on wire rack. Sprinkle with powdered sugar just before serving.

CARROT OAT MUFFINS

MAKES 12 MUFFINS

¾ cup plus 2 tablespoons old-fashioned oats

¾ cup whole wheat flour

¾ cup all-purpose flour

⅓ cup sugar

1½ teaspoons baking powder

1 teaspoon ground cinnamon

½ teaspoon baking soda

¼ teaspoon salt

½ cup milk

½ cup unsweetened applesauce

2 eggs, beaten

2 tablespoons canola oil

½ cup shredded carrot (1 medium to large carrot)

¼ cup finely chopped walnuts (optional)

1. Preheat oven to 350°F. Spray 12 standard (2½-inch) muffin cups with nonstick cooking spray or line with paper baking cups.

2. Combine oats, whole wheat flour, all-purpose flour, sugar, baking powder, cinnamon, baking soda and salt in medium bowl; mix well.

3. Whisk milk, applesauce, eggs and oil in large bowl until well blended. Stir in carrot. Add flour mixture; stir just until moistened. Spoon batter evenly into prepared muffin cups; sprinkle with walnuts, if desired.

4. Bake 20 to 22 minutes or until golden brown. Cool in pan 5 minutes; remove to wire rack to cool completely.

NOTE: These muffins are best eaten the same day.

PUMPKIN SPICE MINI DOUGHNUTS

MAKES 36 DOUGHNUTS

- 1 tablespoon granulated sugar
- 2 teaspoons ground cinnamon, divided
- 2 cups white whole wheat flour
- ½ cup packed brown sugar
- 1½ teaspoons baking powder
- ½ teaspoon salt
- ½ teaspoon ground ginger
- ½ teaspoon ground nutmeg
- ¼ teaspoon baking soda
- 2 eggs
- ½ cup solid-pack pumpkin
- ¼ cup (½ stick) butter, softened
- ¼ cup milk
- 1 teaspoon vanilla

1. Preheat oven to 350°F. Spray 36 mini (1¾-inch) muffin cups with nonstick cooking spray. Combine granulated sugar and 1 teaspoon cinnamon in shallow bowl; set aside.

2. Combine flour, brown sugar, baking powder, remaining 1 teaspoon cinnamon, salt, ginger, nutmeg and baking soda in medium bowl; mix well. Beat eggs, pumpkin, butter, milk and vanilla in large bowl with electric mixer at medium speed until well blended. Gradually add flour mixture; beat just until blended. Spoon scant tablespoonful batter into each prepared muffin cup.

3. Bake 12 minutes or until toothpick inserted into centers comes out clean. Cool in pans 2 minutes.

4. Working with one doughnut at a time, roll in cinnamon-sugar to coat. Cool slightly on wire racks. Serve warm or cool completely.

QUICK CHOCOLATE CHIP STICKY BUNS

MAKES 8 STICKY BUNS

2 tablespoons butter

1 package (11 ounces) refrigerated French bread dough

¼ cup sugar

1 teaspoon ground cinnamon

½ cup mini semisweet chocolate chips

⅓ cup pecan pieces, toasted*

1 tablespoon maple syrup

*To toast pecans, spread on baking sheet. Bake in preheated 350°F oven 6 to 8 minutes or until lightly browned and fragrant, stirring frequently.

1. Preheat oven to 350°F. Place butter in 9-inch round cake pan; place pan in oven while preheating to melt butter.

2. Meanwhile, unroll dough on cutting board or clean work surface. Combine sugar and cinnamon in small bowl; sprinkle evenly over dough. Sprinkle with chocolate chips. Starting with short side, roll up dough jelly-roll style. Cut crosswise into 8 slices with serrated knife.

3. Remove cake pan from oven. Stir pecans and maple syrup into melted butter; mix well. Arrange dough slices cut sides up in pan, pressing gently into pecan mixture.

4. Bake 20 to 22 minutes or until golden brown. Immediately invert pan onto serving plate; scrape any pecans or butter mixture remaining in pan onto sticky buns. Serve warm.

CRANBERRY ORANGE COFFEECAKE

MAKES 12 SERVINGS

1½ cups biscuit baking mix

⅓ cup granulated sugar

⅓ cup sour cream

1 egg

2 tablespoons orange juice

1 tablespoon plus
   1 teaspoon grated
   orange peel, divided

1 teaspoon vanilla

1 cup fresh or frozen
   whole cranberries

½ cup chopped dried fruit
   (such as apricots,
   golden raisins and figs)

⅓ cup coarsely chopped
   walnuts

½ cup packed brown sugar

2 tablespoons butter,
   softened

1. Preheat oven to 350°F. Spray 12-inch tart pan with removable bottom with nonstick cooking spray.

2. Combine baking mix and granulated sugar in large bowl; mix well. Whisk sour cream, egg, orange juice, 1 tablespoon orange peel and vanilla in medium bowl until well blended. Add to baking mix; stir just until moistened. Spread batter in prepared pan; sprinkle with cranberries, dried fruit and walnuts.

3. Combine brown sugar, butter and remaining 1 teaspoon orange peel in small bowl; mix well. Sprinkle over top of tart.

4. Bake 25 to 30 minutes or until lightly browned. Serve warm or cool completely on wire rack.

BREAKFAST SAUSAGE MONKEY MUFFINS

MAKES 12 MUFFINS

12 ounces bulk pork
   sausage

1 egg, beaten

1½ cups (6 ounces)
   shredded Mexican
   cheese blend, divided

2 packages (7½ ounces
   each) refrigerated
   buttermilk biscuits
   (10 biscuits per
   package)

1. Preheat oven to 350°F. Spray 12 standard (2½-inch) muffin cups with nonstick cooking spray.

2. Cook and stir sausage in large skillet over medium-high heat about 8 minutes or until no longer pink, breaking apart any large pieces. Spoon sausage and drippings into large bowl; let cool 2 minutes. Add egg; stir until blended. Stir in 1¼ cups cheese.

3. Separate biscuits; cut each biscuit into 4 pieces with scissors. Roll biscuit pieces in sausage mixture to coat; place 6 to 7 biscuit pieces in each muffin cup. Sprinkle with remaining ¼ cup cheese.

4. Bake about 22 minutes or until golden brown. Remove muffins to paper towel-lined plate. Serve warm.

CRANBERRY PUMPKIN NUT BREAD

MAKES 10 TO 12 SERVINGS

2 cups all-purpose flour

2 teaspoons pumpkin pie spice

1 teaspoon baking powder

½ teaspoon baking soda

½ teaspoon salt

1 cup solid-pack pumpkin

¾ cup granulated sugar

½ cup packed brown sugar

2 eggs

⅓ cup vegetable or canola oil

1 cup chopped dried cranberries

¾ cup chopped macadamia nuts, toasted*

*To toast macadamia nuts, spread on baking sheet. Bake in preheated 350°F oven 8 to 10 minutes or until lightly browned and fragrant, stirring frequently.

1. Preheat oven to 350°F. Spray 9×5-inch loaf pan with nonstick cooking spray.

2. Combine flour, pumpkin pie spice, baking powder, baking soda and salt in large bowl; mix well.

3. Whisk pumpkin, granulated sugar, brown sugar, eggs and oil in medium bowl until well blended. Add to flour mixture; stir just until moistened. Stir in cranberries and nuts. Pour batter into prepared pan.

4. Bake 45 to 50 minutes or until toothpick inserted into center comes out clean. Cool in pan 15 minutes; remove to wire rack to cool completely.

APPLE BUTTER SPICE MUFFINS

MAKES 12 MUFFINS

½ cup sugar

1 teaspoon ground cinnamon

¼ teaspoon ground nutmeg

⅛ teaspoon ground allspice

½ cup pecans or walnuts, chopped

2 cups all-purpose flour

2 teaspoons baking powder

¼ teaspoon salt

1 cup milk

¼ cup vegetable oil

1 egg

¼ cup apple butter

1. Preheat oven to 400°F. Line 12 standard (2½-inch) muffin cups with paper baking cups.

2. Combine sugar, cinnamon, nutmeg and allspice in large bowl; mix well. Remove 2 tablespoons sugar mixture to small bowl; toss with pecans until coated. Add flour, baking powder and salt to remaining sugar mixture.

3. Whisk milk, oil and egg in medium bowl until well blended. Add to flour mixture; stir just until moistened. Spoon 1 tablespoon batter into each prepared muffin cup. Top with 1 teaspoon apple butter; spoon remaining batter evenly over apple butter. Sprinkle with pecan mixture.

4. Bake 20 to 25 minutes or until golden brown and toothpick inserted into centers comes out clean. Remove to wire rack to cool 10 minutes. Serve warm or cool completely.

COOKIES & BARS

GINGERY OAT AND MOLASSES COOKIES

MAKES ABOUT 48 COOKIES

1 cup all-purpose flour

¾ cup whole wheat flour

½ cup old-fashioned oats

1½ teaspoons baking powder

1½ teaspoons ground ginger

1 teaspoon baking soda

½ teaspoon ground cinnamon

¼ teaspoon salt

¾ cup sugar

½ cup (1 stick) butter, softened

1 egg

¼ cup molasses

¼ teaspoon vanilla

1 cup chopped crystallized ginger

½ cup chopped walnuts

1. Combine all-purpose flour, whole wheat flour, oats, baking powder, ground ginger, baking soda, cinnamon and salt in medium bowl; mix well. Beat sugar and butter in large bowl with electric mixer at high speed until light and fluffy. Beat in egg, molasses and vanilla. Gradually add flour mixture; beat at low speed until blended. Stir in crystallized ginger and walnuts.

2. Shape dough into 2 (8- to 10-inch) logs. Wrap with plastic wrap; refrigerate 1 to 3 hours.

3. Preheat oven to 350°F. Line cookie sheets with parchment paper or spray with nonstick cooking spray.

4. Cut logs into ⅓-inch slices; place 1½ inches apart on prepared cookie sheets.

5. Bake 12 to 14 minutes or until set. Cool on cookie sheets 5 minutes; remove to wire racks to cool completely.

PUMPKIN CHEESECAKE BARS

MAKES 24 BARS

1½ cups gingersnap crumbs, plus additional for garnish

6 tablespoons (¾ stick) butter, melted

2 eggs

¼ cup plus 2 tablespoons sugar, divided

2½ teaspoons vanilla, divided

11 ounces cream cheese, softened

1¼ cups solid-pack pumpkin

1 teaspoon ground cinnamon

¼ teaspoon ground ginger

¼ teaspoon ground nutmeg

¼ teaspoon ground cloves

1 cup sour cream

1. Preheat oven to 325°F. Spray 13×9-inch baking pan with nonstick cooking spray.

2. Combine 1½ cups gingersnap crumbs and butter in small bowl; mix well. Press into bottom of prepared pan. Bake 10 minutes.

3. Meanwhile, combine eggs, ¼ cup sugar and 1½ teaspoons vanilla in food processor or blender; process 1 minute or until smooth. Add cream cheese and pumpkin; process until well blended. Stir in cinnamon, ginger, nutmeg and cloves. Pour evenly over hot crust.

4. Bake 40 minutes. Whisk sour cream, remaining 2 tablespoons sugar and 1 teaspoon vanilla in small bowl until blended. Remove cheesecake from oven; spread sour cream mixture evenly over top. Bake 5 minutes. Turn off oven; open door halfway and let cheesecake cool completely in oven. Refrigerate at least 2 hours before serving. Garnish with additional gingersnap crumbs.

CRANBERRY COCONUT BARS

MAKES 24 BARS

2 cups fresh or frozen cranberries

1 cup dried sweetened cranberries

⅔ cup granulated sugar

¼ cup water

Grated peel of 1 lemon

1¼ cups all-purpose flour

¾ cup old-fashioned oats

½ teaspoon baking soda

½ teaspoon salt

1 cup packed brown sugar

¾ cup (1½ sticks) butter, softened

1 cup shredded sweetened coconut

1 cup chopped pecans, toasted*

*To toast pecans, spread on baking sheet. Bake in preheated 350°F oven 5 to 7 minutes or until lightly browned and fragrant, stirring frequently.

1. Preheat oven to 400°F. Grease and flour 13×9-inch baking pan.

2. Combine fresh cranberries, dried cranberries, granulated sugar, water and lemon peel in medium saucepan; cook over medium-high heat 10 to 15 minutes or until cranberries begin to pop, stirring frequently. Mash cranberries with back of spoon. Let stand 10 minutes.

3. Combine flour, oats, baking soda and salt in medium bowl; mix well. Beat brown sugar and butter in large bowl with electric mixer at medium speed until creamy. Add flour mixture; beat just until blended. Stir in coconut and pecans. Reserve 1½ cups for topping; press remaining crumb mixture into bottom of prepared pan. Bake 10 minutes.

4. Gently spread cranberry filling evenly over crust. Sprinkle with reserved crumb mixture.

5. Bake 18 to 20 minutes or until center is set and top is golden brown. Cool completely in pan on wire rack.

NOTE: When fresh or frozen cranberries aren't available, you can make these bars with dried cranberries. Prepare the filling using 2 cups dried sweetened cranberries, 1 cup water and the grated peel of 1 lemon; cook 8 to 10 minutes over medium heat, stirring frequently. Use the filling as directed in step 4.

ROSEMARY HONEY SHORTBREAD COOKIES

MAKES 24 COOKIES

2 cups all-purpose flour

1 tablespoon fresh rosemary leaves,* minced

½ teaspoon salt

½ teaspoon baking powder

¾ cup (1½ sticks) butter, softened

½ cup powdered sugar

2 tablespoons honey

*For best flavor, use only fresh rosemary.

1. Combine flour, rosemary, salt and baking powder in medium bowl; mix well.

2. Beat butter, powdered sugar and honey in large bowl with electric mixer at medium speed until creamy. Add flour mixture; beat at low speed just until blended. (Mixture will be crumbly.)

3. Shape dough into a log. Wrap with plastic wrap; refrigerate 1 hour or until firm. (Dough can be refrigerated up to several days before baking.)

4. Preheat oven to 350°F. Line cookie sheets with parchment paper. Cut log into ½-inch slices; place 2 inches apart on prepared cookie sheets.

5. Bake 13 minutes or until set. Cool on cookie sheets 1 minute; remove to wire racks to cool completely.

CHOCOLATE PECAN BARS

MAKES 24 BARS

CRUST

1⅓ cups all-purpose flour

½ cup (1 stick) butter, softened

¼ cup packed brown sugar

½ teaspoon salt

TOPPING

¾ cup light corn syrup

3 eggs, lightly beaten

2 tablespoons butter, melted

½ teaspoon vanilla

½ teaspoon almond extract

¾ cup milk chocolate chips

¾ cup semisweet chocolate chips

¾ cup chopped pecans, toasted*

¾ cup granulated sugar

*To toast pecans, spread on baking sheet. Bake in preheated 350°F oven 5 to 7 minutes or until lightly browned and fragrant, stirring frequently.

1. Preheat oven to 350°F. Spray 13×9-inch baking pan with nonstick cooking spray.

2. For crust, combine flour, ½ cup butter, brown sugar and salt in medium bowl; mix with fork until crumbly. Press into bottom of prepared pan. Bake 12 to 15 minutes or until lightly browned. Remove to wire rack to cool 10 minutes.

3. Meanwhile, for topping, combine corn syrup, eggs, 2 tablespoons butter, vanilla and almond extract in large bowl; stir with fork until combined (do not beat). Fold in chocolate chips, pecans and granulated sugar until blended. Pour over baked crust.

4. Bake 25 to 30 minutes or until toothpick inserted into center comes out clean. Cool completely in pan on wire rack.

MULTIGRAIN WHITE CHOCOLATE CRANBERRY COOKIES

MAKES ABOUT 72 COOKIES

2 cups whole wheat flour

1½ cups uncooked five-grain cereal

1 teaspoon baking soda

½ teaspoon salt

¾ cup packed brown sugar

¾ cup canola oil

⅓ cup granulated sugar

2 eggs

1 tablespoon vanilla

1 cup dried cranberries

½ cup white chocolate chips

1. Preheat oven to 375°F.

2. Combine flour, cereal, baking soda and salt in medium bowl; mix well. Whisk brown sugar, oil, granulated sugar, eggs and vanilla in large bowl. Add flour mixture; stir until blended. Stir in cranberries and white chips. Drop dough by rounded teaspoonfuls onto ungreased cookie sheets.

3. Bake 8 to 10 minutes or until golden brown but soft in center. Cool on cookie sheets 1 minute; remove to wire racks to cool completely.

NEW ENGLAND RAISIN SPICE COOKIES

MAKES ABOUT 60 COOKIES

2¼ cups all-purpose flour

2 teaspoons baking soda

1 teaspoon salt

¾ teaspoon ground cinnamon

¼ teaspoon ground ginger

¼ teaspoon ground cloves

⅛ teaspoon ground allspice

1½ cups raisins

1 cup packed brown sugar

½ cup shortening

¼ cup (½ stick) butter, softened

1 egg

⅓ cup molasses

Granulated sugar

1. Combine flour, baking soda, salt, cinnamon, ginger, cloves and allspice in medium bowl; mix well. Stir in raisins. Beat brown sugar, shortening and butter in large bowl with electric mixer at medium speed until creamy. Add egg and molasses; beat until fluffy. Gradually add flour mixture; beat at low speed just until blended. Cover and refrigerate at least 2 hours.

2. Preheat oven to 350°F. Shape heaping tablespoons of dough into balls. Roll in granulated sugar. Place 2 inches apart on ungreased cookie sheets.

3. Bake 8 minutes or until golden brown. Cool on cookie sheets 1 minute; remove to wire racks to cool completely.

SOUTHERN CARAMEL APPLE BARS

MAKES 24 BARS

2 cups all-purpose flour

1 teaspoon salt

½ teaspoon baking powder

½ teaspoon baking soda

⅔ cup butter

¾ cup packed brown sugar

½ cup granulated sugar

1 egg

1 teaspoon vanilla

4 Granny Smith apples, peeled and coarsely chopped

½ cup pecans, chopped

24 caramel candies, unwrapped

2 tablespoons milk

1. Preheat oven to 350°F. Spray 13×9-inch baking pan with nonstick cooking spray.

2. Combine flour, salt, baking powder and baking soda in medium bowl; mix well. Melt butter in medium saucepan over medium heat. Remove from heat; stir in brown sugar and granulated sugar. Add egg and vanilla; stir until well blended. Add flour mixture; stir until blended. Press into bottom of prepared pan; top with apples.

3. Bake 40 to 45 minutes or until edges are browned and pulling away from sides of pan. Cool completely in pan on wire rack.

4. Toast pecans in medium nonstick skillet over medium-high heat 2 minutes or until fragrant, stirring frequently. Remove from skillet; set aside. Wipe out skillet with paper towel. Heat caramels and milk in same skillet over medium-low heat until melted and smooth, stirring constantly.

5. Drizzle caramel sauce over cooled bars; sprinkle with pecans. Let stand 30 minutes before cutting.

WHOLE WHEAT PUMPKIN BARS

MAKES 24 BARS

1 cup all-purpose flour

1 cup whole wheat flour

¾ cup sugar

1½ teaspoons baking powder

1½ teaspoons ground cinnamon

1 teaspoon baking soda

¾ teaspoon salt

½ teaspoon ground ginger

½ teaspoon ground nutmeg

1 can (15 ounces) solid-pack pumpkin

¾ cup canola oil

2 eggs

2 tablespoons molasses

Cream Cheese Frosting (recipe follows)

½ cup mini semisweet chocolate chips

1. Preheat oven to 350°F. Spray 13×9-inch baking pan with nonstick cooking spray.

2. Combine all-purpose flour, whole wheat flour, sugar, baking powder, cinnamon, baking soda, salt, ginger and nutmeg in medium bowl; mix well.

3. Whisk pumpkin, oil, eggs and molasses in large bowl until well blended. Add flour mixture; stir until blended. Spread batter in prepared pan. (Batter will be very thick.)

4. Bake 20 to 25 minutes or until toothpick inserted into center comes out clean. Cool completely in pan on wire rack.

5. Prepare Cream Cheese Frosting. Spread frosting over bars; sprinkle with chocolate chips.

CREAM CHEESE FROSTING: Beat 4 ounces softened cream cheese and ½ cup (1 stick) softened butter in medium bowl with electric mixer at medium-high speed until creamy. Add 2 cups powdered sugar; beat at low speed until blended. Add 1 tablespoon milk; beat at medium-high speed 2 to 3 minutes or until frosting is light and fluffy.

CRANBERRY WALNUT GRANOLA BARS

MAKES 12 BARS

2 packages (3 ounces each) ramen noodles, any flavor,* broken into small pieces

¾ cup all-purpose flour

1 teaspoon pumpkin pie spice

½ teaspoon baking soda

½ teaspoon salt

1 cup packed brown sugar

¼ cup (½ stick) butter, softened

2 eggs

¼ cup orange juice

1 cup chopped walnuts

½ cup dried cranberries

*Discard seasoning packets.

1. Preheat oven to 350°F. Spray 9-inch square baking pan with nonstick cooking spray.

2. Combine noodles, flour, pumpkin pie spice, baking soda and salt in medium bowl; mix well.

3. Beat brown sugar and butter in large bowl with electric mixer at medium speed until light and fluffy. Add eggs and orange juice; beat until blended. Gradually add noodle mixture, beating at low speed just until combined. Stir in walnuts and cranberries. Spread batter in prepared pan.

4. Bake 20 to 25 minutes or until toothpick inserted into center comes out clean. Cool completely in pan on wire rack.

PUMPKIN WHITE CHOCOLATE DROPS

MAKES ABOUT 36 COOKIES

1 cup granulated sugar

1 cup (2 sticks) butter, softened

½ (15-ounce) can solid-pack pumpkin

1 egg

2 cups all-purpose flour

1 teaspoon pumpkin pie spice*

½ teaspoon baking powder

¼ teaspoon baking soda

1 cup white chocolate chips

1 cup prepared cream cheese frosting

*Or substitute ½ teaspoon ground cinnamon, ¼ teaspoon ground ginger, ⅛ teaspoon ground allspice and ⅛ teaspoon ground nutmeg.

1. Preheat oven to 375°F. Line cookie sheets with parchment paper or spray with nonstick cooking spray.

2. Beat granulated sugar and butter in large bowl with electric mixer at medium speed until light and fluffy. Add pumpkin and egg; beat until well blended. Add flour, pumpkin pie spice, baking powder and baking soda; beat just until blended. Stir in white chips. Drop dough by tablespoonfuls about 2 inches apart onto prepared cookie sheets.

3. Bake 16 minutes or until set and lightly browned. Cool on cookie sheets 1 minute; remove to wire racks to cool completely.

4. Spread frosting over cookies.

FRUIT AND PECAN BROWNIES

MAKES 12 BROWNIES

1 cup sugar

½ cup (1 stick) butter, softened

2 eggs

2 ounces unsweetened chocolate, melted

1 teaspoon vanilla

½ cup all-purpose flour

1 cup chopped dried mixed fruit

1 cup coarsely chopped pecans, divided

1 cup (6 ounces) semisweet chocolate chips, divided

1. Preheat oven to 350°F. Spray 8-inch square baking pan with nonstick cooking spray.

2. Beat sugar and butter in large bowl with electric mixer at medium speed until light and fluffy. Add eggs, one at a time, beating until blended after each addition. Beat in melted chocolate and vanilla. Stir in flour, dried fruit, ½ cup pecans and ½ cup chocolate chips. Spread batter evenly in prepared pan; sprinkle with remaining ½ cup pecans and ½ cup chocolate chips.

3. Bake 25 to 30 minutes or just until center feels firm. Cover brownies with waxed paper or foil; cool completely in pan on wire rack.

CAKES &
CHEESECAKES

TOFFEE CRUNCH CHEESECAKE

MAKES 10 TO 12 SERVINGS

8 ounces chocolate cookies or vanilla wafers, crushed

¼ cup (½ stick) butter, melted

3 packages (8 ounces each) cream cheese, softened

½ cup granulated sugar

¼ cup packed brown sugar

3 eggs

1¾ cups (10-ounce package) toffee baking bits, divided

1¼ teaspoons vanilla

Sweetened whipped cream

1. Preheat oven to 350°F. Combine cookie crumbs and butter in medium bowl; mix well. Press firmly into bottom of 9-inch springform pan.

2. Beat cream cheese, granulated sugar and brown sugar in large bowl with electric mixer at medium speed until smooth. Add eggs, one at a time, beating well after each addition. Reserve 1 tablespoon toffee bits; gently stir remaining toffee bits and vanilla into batter. Pour into crust.

3. Bake 45 to 50 minutes or until almost set. Remove to wire rack; carefully run knife around edge of pan to loosen cheesecake. Cool completely; remove side of pan. Cover and refrigerate until cold.

4. Just before serving, top with whipped cream and reserved toffee bits.

ICED PUMPKIN BITES

MAKES 24 MINI CUPCAKES

¾ cup solid-pack pumpkin

½ cup packed brown sugar

½ cup milk

⅓ cup vegetable oil

1 egg

1 teaspoon vanilla

1¾ cups all-purpose flour

2 teaspoons baking powder

2 teaspoons ground cinnamon, divided

½ teaspoon ground nutmeg

½ teaspoon salt

1 cup powdered sugar

⅓ cup maple syrup

¼ cup granulated sugar

1. Preheat oven to 350°F. Spray 24 mini (1¾-cup) muffin cups with nonstick cooking spray.

2. Whisk pumpkin, brown sugar, milk, oil, egg and vanilla in large bowl until well blended. Add flour, baking powder, 1 teaspoon cinnamon, nutmeg and salt; stir just until combined. Scoop heaping tablespoonfuls of batter into prepared muffin cups.

3. Bake 12 minutes or until toothpick inserted into centers comes out clean. Cool in pans 5 minutes; remove to wire racks.

4. Combine powdered sugar and maple syrup in small microwavable bowl; microwave on HIGH 30 seconds. Stir until well blended and smooth. Dip tops of cupcakes into syrup mixture; return to wire racks to set.

5. Combine granulated sugar and remaining 1 teaspoon cinnamon in small bowl; sprinkle over cupcakes.

CRANBERRY POUND CAKE

MAKES 12 SERVINGS

1½ cups sugar

1 cup (2 sticks) butter, softened

¼ teaspoon salt

¼ teaspoon ground mace

4 eggs

2 cups cake flour

1 cup chopped fresh or frozen cranberries

1. Preheat oven to 350°F. Grease and flour 9×5-inch loaf pan.

2. Beat sugar, butter, salt and mace in large bowl with electric mixer at medium speed until light and fluffy. Add eggs, one at a time, beating well after each addition. Add flour, ½ cup at a time, beating at low speed until blended. Fold in cranberries. Spoon batter into prepared pan.

3. Bake 60 to 70 minutes or until toothpick inserted into center comes out clean. Cool in pan 5 minutes. Run knife around edges of pan to loosen cake; cool 30 minutes. Remove from pan; cool completely on wire rack.

NOTE: When fresh or frozen cranberries aren't available, you can make this cake with dried cranberries. Cover 1 cup dried cranberries with hot water and let stand 10 minutes. Drain well before using.

APPLE CAKE

2½ cups all-purpose flour

2 teaspoons ground cinnamon, divided

1 teaspoon baking powder

1 teaspoon baking soda

1 teaspoon salt

¼ teaspoon ground nutmeg

1¼ cups granulated sugar, divided

1 cup (2 sticks) butter, softened

¾ cup packed brown sugar

2 eggs

1 teaspoon vanilla

1 cup buttermilk

3 cups chopped peeled apples

1 cup chopped nuts

1. Preheat oven to 350°F. Spray 13×9-inch baking pan with nonstick cooking spray.

2. Combine flour, 1 teaspoon cinnamon, baking powder, baking soda, salt and nutmeg in medium bowl; mix well.

3. Beat ¾ cup granulated sugar, butter, brown sugar, eggs and vanilla in large bowl with electric mixer at medium speed 3 minutes or until creamy. Beat in buttermilk until well blended. Add flour mixture; beat at low speed until blended. Stir in apples. Pour batter into prepared pan.

4. Combine remaining ½ cup granulated sugar, 1 teaspoon cinnamon and nuts in small bowl; mix well. Sprinkle over batter.

5. Bake 35 to 40 minutes or until toothpick inserted in center comes out clean. Cool completely in pan on wire rack.

CARROT GINGER CUPCAKES

MAKES 24 CUPCAKES

3 cups all-purpose flour

⅓ cup pecan chips

2 teaspoons baking powder

1 teaspoon baking soda

1 teaspoon salt

½ teaspoon ground cinnamon

1½ cups granulated sugar

1¼ cups (2½ sticks) plus 2 tablespoons butter, softened, divided

1 tablespoon honey

4 eggs

1 pound carrots, shredded

Grated peel of 2 oranges

Juice of 1 orange

1 tablespoon plus 1 teaspoon vanilla, divided

1½ teaspoons grated fresh ginger

1 package (8 ounces) cream cheese, softened

1 teaspoon orange extract

3½ cups powdered sugar

Chopped pecans (optional)

1. Preheat oven to 350°F. Line 24 standard (2½-inch) muffin cups with paper baking cups.

2. Combine flour, pecan chips, baking powder, baking soda, salt and cinnamon in medium bowl; mix well. Beat granulated sugar, 1 cup plus 2 tablespoons butter and honey in large bowl with electric mixer at medium speed until light and fluffy. Add eggs, one at a time, beating well after each addition. Add carrots, orange peel, orange juice, 1 tablespoon vanilla and ginger; beat until blended. Add flour mixture; stir just until combined. Spoon batter evenly into prepared muffin cups.

3. Bake 20 minutes or until toothpick inserted into centers comes out clean. Cool in pans 10 minutes; remove to wire racks to cool completely.

4. Meanwhile, beat cream cheese, remaining ¼ cup butter, 1 teaspoon vanilla and orange extract in medium bowl at medium speed until light and fluffy. Gradually add powdered sugar, beating until well blended.

5. Frost cupcakes; sprinkle with chopped pecans, if desired. Refrigerate until ready to serve.

PEAR SPICE CAKE

MAKES 12 SERVINGS

4 cups chopped peeled
   pears
2 cups granulated sugar
1 cup chopped walnuts
3 cups all-purpose flour
2 teaspoons baking soda
¾ teaspoon ground
   cinnamon
½ teaspoon salt
¼ teaspoon ground nutmeg
⅛ teaspoon ground cloves
1 cup vegetable oil
2 eggs
1½ teaspoons vanilla
   Powdered sugar
   (optional)

1. Combine pears, granulated sugar and walnuts in medium bowl; mix well. Let stand 1 hour, stirring occasionally.

2. Preheat oven to 375°F. Grease and flour 12-cup (10-inch) bundt or tube pan.

3. Combine flour, baking soda, cinnamon, salt, nutmeg and cloves in medium bowl; mix well.

4. Beat oil, eggs and vanilla in large bowl until well blended. Add flour mixture; beat until blended. Stir in pear mixture. Pour batter into prepared pan.

5. Bake 1 hour 10 minutes or until toothpick inserted near center comes out clean. Cool in pan 20 minutes. Loosen edge of cake; invert onto wire rack to cool completely. Sprinkle with powdered sugar, if desired.

MOLTEN CINNAMON-CHOCOLATE CAKES

MAKES 6 CAKES

6 ounces semisweet chocolate

¾ cup (1½ sticks) butter

1½ cups powdered sugar, plus additional for serving

4 eggs

6 tablespoons all-purpose flour

1½ teaspoons vanilla

¾ teaspoon ground cinnamon

1. Preheat oven to 425°F. Spray 6 jumbo muffin cups or 6 (1-cup) custard cups with nonstick cooking spray.

2. Combine chocolate and butter in medium microwavable bowl; microwave on HIGH 1½ minutes or until melted and smooth, stirring every 30 seconds.

3. Whisk in 1½ cups powdered sugar, eggs, flour, vanilla and cinnamon until well blended. Pour batter evenly into prepared muffin cups.

4. Bake 13 minutes or until cakes spring back when lightly touched but centers are soft. Let stand 1 minute. Loosen sides of cakes with knife; gently lift out and invert onto serving plates. Sprinkle with additional powdered sugar. Serve immediately.

PUMPKIN CINNAMON CHIP CAKE

MAKES 12 TO 16 SERVINGS

1 package (about 15 ounces) yellow cake mix

1 can (15 ounces) solid-pack pumpkin

2 eggs

½ cup water

2 teaspoons pumpkin pie spice

½ cup cinnamon chips, divided

½ cup chopped pecans, divided

1. Preheat oven to 350°F. Spray 13×9-inch baking pan with nonstick cooking spray.

2. Beat cake mix, pumpkin, eggs, water and pumpkin pie spice in large bowl with electric mixer 1 to 2 minutes or until well blended. Stir in ¼ cup cinnamon chips and ¼ cup pecans. Spread batter in prepared pan; sprinkle with remaining cinnamon chips and pecans.

3. Bake 25 to 30 minutes or until toothpick inserted into center comes out clean. Cool in pan at least 15 minutes before serving.

MAPLE-SWEET POTATO MINI CHEESECAKES

MAKES 12 SERVINGS

12 mini graham cracker
   crusts

 1 package (8 ounces)
   cream cheese, softened

½ cup vanilla yogurt

 1 can (16 ounces) sweet
   potatoes, drained
   and mashed (see Tip)

½ cup pure maple syrup

 1 teaspoon vanilla

½ teaspoon ground
   cinnamon

¼ teaspoon ground cloves

 1 egg

 1 egg white

12 pecan halves

1. Preheat oven to 350°F. Place crusts on large baking sheet.

2. Beat cream cheese in large bowl with electric mixer at medium speed until creamy. Beat in yogurt until smooth. Add sweet potatoes, maple syrup, vanilla, cinnamon and cloves; beat until smooth. Beat in egg and egg white until blended.

3. Spoon about ⅓ cup sweet potato mixture into each crust; top with pecan half.

4. Bake 30 to 35 minutes or until set and knife inserted into centers comes out clean. Remove to wire rack to cool 1 hour. Refrigerate before serving.

TIP: Mashing sweet potatoes by hand produces pie filling with a somewhat coarse texture. For a smoother texture, process the sweet potatoes in a food processor.

VARIATION: For one larger cheesecake, pour the sweet potato mixture into a 9-inch graham cracker crust. Bake 40 to 45 minutes or until a knife inserted into the center comes out clean.

GLAZED APPLESAUCE SPICE CAKE

MAKES 12 SERVINGS

2¼ cups all-purpose flour

2 teaspoons baking soda

2 teaspoons ground
   cinnamon

¾ teaspoon ground nutmeg

½ teaspoon ground ginger

¼ teaspoon salt

1 cup packed brown sugar

¾ cup (1½ sticks) butter,
   softened

3 eggs

1½ teaspoons vanilla

1½ cups unsweetened
   applesauce

½ cup milk

⅔ cup chopped walnuts

⅔ cup butterscotch chips

Apple Glaze
   (recipe follows)

1. Preheat oven to 350°F. Grease and flour 12-cup (10-inch) bundt pan.

2. Combine flour, baking soda, cinnamon, nutmeg, ginger and salt in medium bowl; mix well.

3. Beat brown sugar and butter in large bowl with electric mixer at medium speed until light and fluffy. Beat in eggs and vanilla until well blended. Add flour mixture alternately with applesauce and milk, beginning and ending with flour mixture, beating well after each addition. Stir in walnuts and butterscotch chips. Pour batter into prepared pan.

4. Bake 45 to 50 minutes or until toothpick inserted near center comes out clean. Cool in pan 15 minutes; invert onto wire rack to cool completely.

5. Prepare Apple Glaze; spoon over top of cake. Store tightly covered at room temperature.

APPLE GLAZE: Place 1 cup sifted powdered sugar in small bowl. Stir in 2 to 3 tablespoons apple juice concentrate to make stiff glaze.

OAT-APRICOT SNACK CAKE

MAKES 12 TO 16 SERVINGS

1 cup all-purpose flour

½ cup whole wheat flour

1 teaspoon baking soda

1 teaspoon ground cinnamon

½ teaspoon salt

1 container (6 ounces) plain yogurt (not fat free)

¾ cup packed brown sugar

½ cup granulated sugar

⅓ cup vegetable oil

1 egg

2 tablespoons milk

2 teaspoons vanilla

2 cups old-fashioned oats

1 cup (about 6 ounces) chopped dried apricots

1 cup powdered sugar

2 tablespoons milk

1. Preheat oven to 350°F. Spray 13×9-inch baking pan with nonstick cooking spray.

2. Sift all-purpose flour, whole wheat flour, baking soda, cinnamon and salt into medium bowl.

3. Whisk yogurt, brown sugar, granulated sugar, oil, egg, milk and vanilla in large bowl until well blended. Add flour mixture; stir until blended. Stir in oats and apricots. Spread batter in prepared pan.

4. Bake 25 to 30 minutes or until toothpick inserted into center comes out clean. Cool completely in pan on wire rack.

5. Combine powdered sugar and milk in small bowl; whisk until smooth. Spoon glaze into small resealable food storage bag; seal bag. Cut ¼ inch from one corner of bag; drizzle glaze over cake.

PUMPKIN LAYER CAKE

MAKES 12 SERVINGS

2¾ cups all-purpose flour

1 tablespoon baking powder

1½ teaspoons baking soda

1½ teaspoons ground cinnamon

½ teaspoon salt

¼ teaspoon ground allspice

¼ teaspoon ground nutmeg

⅛ teaspoon ground ginger

1½ cups solid-pack pumpkin

1 cup buttermilk*

1½ cups granulated sugar

¾ cup (1½ sticks) butter

3 eggs

Vanilla Maple Frosting (recipe follows)

*Or substitute 1 tablespoon vinegar or lemon juice and enough milk to equal 1 cup. Stir; let stand 5 minutes.

1. Preheat oven to 350°F. Grease and flour 2 (9-inch) round cake pans.

2. Sift flour, baking powder, baking soda, cinnamon, salt, allspice, nutmeg and ginger into medium bowl. Whisk pumpkin and buttermilk in separate medium bowl until well blended.

3. Beat granulated sugar and butter in large bowl with electric mixer at medium speed until light and fluffy. Add eggs, one at a time, beating well after each addition. Add flour mixture alternately with pumpkin mixture, beating well after each addition. Pour batter into prepared pans.

4. Bake 40 to 45 minutes or until toothpick inserted into centers comes out clean. Cool in pans 10 minutes; remove to wire racks to cool completely.

5. Prepare Vanilla Maple Frosting; fill and frost cake with frosting.

VANILLA MAPLE FROSTING: Beat 1 cup (2 sticks) softened butter in large bowl with electric mixer at medium-high speed until light and fluffy. Add 1 teaspoon vanilla and ½ teaspoon maple flavoring; beat until well blended. Gradually add 4 cups powdered sugar; beat until light and fluffy.

PIES & TARTS

SHORTCUT PECAN PIE

MAKES 8 SERVINGS

½ (16-ounce) package refrigerated sugar cookie dough

¼ cup all-purpose flour

3 eggs

¾ cup dark corn syrup

¾ cup sugar

1 teaspoon vanilla

¼ teaspoon salt

2 cups chopped pecans

1. Preheat oven to 350°F. Lightly spray 9-inch pie plate with nonstick cooking spray. Let cookie dough stand at room temperature about 15 minutes.

2. Beat cookie dough and flour in large bowl with electric mixer at medium speed until well blended. Press dough evenly onto bottom and ½ inch up side of prepared pie plate. Crimp edge with fork. Bake 20 minutes.

3. Meanwhile, whisk eggs in large bowl. Add corn syrup, sugar, vanilla and salt; whisk until well blended. Pour over crust; sprinkle evenly with pecans.

4. Bake 40 to 45 minutes or just until center is set. Cool completely on wire rack.

CRANBERRY PHYLLO CHEESECAKE TARTS

MAKES 12 SERVINGS

1 cup fresh or frozen cranberries

¼ cup plus 1 tablespoon sugar, divided

2 tablespoons orange juice

1 teaspoon grated orange peel

¼ teaspoon ground allspice

Butter-flavored cooking spray

6 sheets phyllo dough, thawed

1 container (8 ounces) whipped cream cheese

1 container (6 ounces) vanilla yogurt

1 teaspoon vanilla

1. Preheat oven to 350°F. Combine cranberries, ¼ cup sugar, orange juice, orange peel and allspice in small saucepan; cook and stir over medium heat until berries pop and mixture thickens. Set aside to cool completely.

2. Spray 12 standard (2½-inch) muffin cups with cooking spray. Cut phyllo dough in half lengthwise, then crosswise into thirds. Spray 1 phyllo square lightly with cooking spray. Top with second square, slightly offsetting corners; spray lightly with cooking spray. Top with third square. Place phyllo stack in 1 prepared muffin cup, pressing into bottom and up side of cup. Repeat with remaining phyllo squares.

3. Bake 3 to 4 minutes or until golden brown. Cool completely in pan on wire rack.

4. Beat cream cheese, yogurt, remaining 1 tablespoon sugar and vanilla in medium bowl with electric mixer at medium speed until smooth. Divide mixture evenly among phyllo cups; top with cranberry mixture.

APPLE-PEAR PRALINE PIE

MAKES 8 SERVINGS

Double-Crust Pie Pastry (recipe follows)

4 cups sliced peeled Granny Smith apples

2 cups sliced peeled pears

¾ cup granulated sugar

¼ cup plus 1 tablespoon all-purpose flour, divided

4 teaspoons ground cinnamon

¼ teaspoon salt

½ cup (1 stick) plus 2 tablespoons butter, divided

1 cup packed brown sugar

1 tablespoon half-and-half or milk

1 cup chopped pecans

1. Prepare Double-Crust Pie Pastry.

2. Combine apples, pears, granulated sugar, ¼ cup flour, cinnamon and salt in large bowl; toss to coat. Let stand 15 minutes.

3. Preheat oven to 350°F. Roll out 1 pastry disc into 11-inch circle on floured surface. Line 9-inch deep-dish pie plate with pastry; sprinkle with remaining 1 tablespoon flour. Spoon apple and pear mixture into crust; dot with 2 tablespoons butter. Roll out remaining pastry disc into 10-inch circle. Place over fruit; seal and flute edge. Cut slits in top crust.

4. Bake 1 hour. Meanwhile, combine remaining ½ cup butter, brown sugar and half-and-half in small saucepan; bring to a boil over medium heat, stirring frequently. Boil 2 minutes, stirring constantly. Remove from heat; stir in pecans.

5. Spread pecan mixture over pie. Cool pie on wire rack 15 minutes. Serve warm or at room temperature.

DOUBLE-CRUST PIE PASTRY: Combine 2½ cups all-purpose flour, 1 teaspoon salt and 1 teaspoon granulated sugar in large bowl. Cut in 1 cup (2 sticks) cold cubed butter with pastry blender or two knives until coarse crumbs form. Drizzle with ⅓ cup cold water, 2 tablespoons at a time, stirring just until dough comes together. Divide dough in half. Shape each half into a disc; wrap with plastic wrap. Refrigerate 30 minutes.

SOUR CREAM CRANBERRY PIE

MAKES 8 SERVINGS

2 eggs

2 egg yolks

1½ cups reduced-fat sour cream

1 cup granulated sugar

½ teaspoon vanilla

¼ teaspoon salt

1 cup dried cranberries

1 unbaked 9-inch pie crust

Powdered sugar (optional)

1. Preheat oven to 350°F.

2. Whisk eggs and egg yolks in large bowl until blended. Add sour cream, granulated sugar, vanilla and salt; whisk until blended. Stir in cranberries. Pour into unbaked crust. Place on rimmed baking sheet.

3. Bake 50 minutes or until set. Cool completely on wire rack. Refrigerate 4 hours or overnight.

4. Sprinkle with powdered sugar just before serving, if desired.

TIP: Do not substitute full-fat or fat-free sour cream in this recipe.

SPICED PUMPKIN PIE

MAKES 8 SERVINGS

Pastry for single-crust
9-inch pie

1 can (15 ounces)
solid-pack pumpkin

¾ cup packed brown sugar

4 eggs, lightly beaten

2 teaspoons ground
cinnamon

¾ teaspoon ground ginger

½ teaspoon ground nutmeg

¼ teaspoon salt

⅛ teaspoon ground cloves

1 cup light cream or
half-and-half

1 teaspoon vanilla

Whipped cream
(optional)

1. Preheat oven to 400°F.

2. Roll out pastry into 13-inch circle on lightly floured surface. Line 9-inch pie plate with pastry; trim and flute edge.

3. Whisk pumpkin and brown sugar in large bowl until well blended. Add eggs, cinnamon, ginger, nutmeg, salt and cloves; whisk until blended. Gradually whisk in cream and vanilla until blended. Pour into crust.

4. Bake 40 to 45 minutes or until knife inserted into center comes out clean. Cool on wire rack. Top with whipped cream, if desired.

SWEDISH APPLE PIE

MAKES 8 SERVINGS

- 4 Granny Smith apples, peeled and sliced
- 1 cup plus 1 tablespoon sugar, divided
- 1 tablespoon ground cinnamon
- ¾ cup (1½ sticks) butter, melted
- 1 cup all-purpose flour
- 1 egg
- ½ cup chopped nuts

1. Preheat oven to 350°F.

2. Spread apples in 9-inch deep-dish pie plate or 9-inch square baking dish. Combine 1 tablespoon sugar and cinnamon in small bowl; sprinkle over apples. Drizzle with butter.

3. Combine remaining 1 cup sugar, flour, egg and nuts in medium bowl; mix well. (Mixture will be thick.) Spread batter over apples.

4. Bake 50 to 55 minutes or until top is golden brown.

CHOCOLATE WALNUT TOFFEE TART

MAKES 10 SERVINGS

2 cups all-purpose flour

1¼ cups plus 3 tablespoons sugar, divided

¾ cup (1½ sticks) butter, cut into small pieces

2 egg yolks

1¼ cups whipping cream

1 teaspoon ground cinnamon

2 teaspoons vanilla

2 cups coarsely chopped walnuts

1¼ cups semisweet chocolate chips or chunks, divided

1. Preheat oven to 325°F. Line rimmed baking sheet with foil.

2. Combine flour and 3 tablespoons sugar in food processor; pulse just until mixed. Scatter butter over flour mixture; process 20 seconds. Add egg yolks; process 10 seconds (mixture may be crumbly). Press dough firmly into ungreased 10-inch tart pan with removable bottom or 9- or 10-inch pie plate. Bake 10 minutes or until surface is no longer shiny.

3. *Increase oven temperature to 375°F.* Combine remaining 1¼ cups sugar, cream and cinnamon in large saucepan; bring to a boil over high heat. Reduce heat to medium-low; simmer 10 minutes, stirring frequently. Remove from heat; stir in vanilla.

4. Sprinkle walnuts and 1 cup chocolate chips evenly over crust. Pour cream mixture over top. Place tart pan on prepared baking sheet.

5. Bake 35 to 40 minutes or until filling is bubbly and crust is lightly browned. Cool completely in pan on wire rack.

6. Place remaining ¼ cup chocolate chips in small resealable food storage bag. Microwave on HIGH 20 seconds; knead bag until chocolate is melted. Cut small hole in one corner of bag; drizzle chocolate over tart.

NOTE: Tart may be made up to 5 days in advance. Cover with plastic wrap and store at room temperature.

CHOCOLATE CHESS PIE

MAKES 8 SERVINGS

4 ounces unsweetened chocolate

3 tablespoons butter

3 eggs

1 egg yolk

1¼ cups sugar

½ cup half-and-half

1 to 2 teaspoons instant coffee granules (see Tip)

¼ teaspoon salt

1 unbaked 9-inch pie crust

Whipped cream

Chocolate-covered coffee beans (optional)

1. Preheat oven to 325°F.

2. Combine chocolate and butter in small heavy saucepan; heat over low heat until melted, stirring frequently. Let stand 15 minutes.

3. Whisk eggs and egg yolk in medium bowl. Add sugar, half-and-half, coffee granules and salt; whisk until blended. Add chocolate mixture; whisk until smooth. Pour into unbaked crust.

4. Bake 35 minutes or until set. Cool completely on wire rack. Refrigerate 2 hours or until ready to serve. Top with whipped cream; garnish with chocolate-covered coffee beans.

TIP: Use 2 teaspoons instant coffee granules for a more pronounced coffee flavor; use a smaller amount if a more subtle coffee flavor is preferred.

RUSTIC CRANBERRY-PEAR GALETTE

MAKES 8 SERVINGS

¼ cup sugar, divided

1 tablespoon plus
   1 teaspoon cornstarch

2 teaspoons ground
   cinnamon or apple pie
   spice

4 cups thinly sliced peeled
   Bartlett pears

¼ cup dried cranberries

1 teaspoon vanilla

¼ teaspoon almond extract
   (optional)

1 refrigerated pie crust
   (half of 15-ounce
   package), at room
   temperature

1 egg white

1 tablespoon water

1. Preheat oven to 450°F. Spray pizza pan or baking sheet with nonstick cooking spray.

2. Reserve 1 teaspoon sugar. Combine remaining sugar, cornstarch and cinnamon in medium bowl; mix well. Add pears, cranberries, vanilla and almond extract, if desired; toss to coat.

3. Place crust on prepared pan. Spoon pear mixture into center of crust, spreading to within 2 inches of edge. Fold edge of crust over pear mixture; overlapping and crimping slightly.

4. Whisk egg white and water in small bowl until well blended. Brush edge of crust with egg white mixture; sprinkle with reserved 1 teaspoon sugar.

5. Bake 25 minutes or until pears are tender and crust is golden brown.* Cool on pan on wire rack 30 minutes. Serve warm.

If edge browns too quickly, cover with foil after 15 minutes of baking.

APPLE BUTTERMILK PIE

MAKES 8 SERVINGS

2 medium Granny Smith apples

3 eggs

1½ cups sugar, divided

1 cup buttermilk

⅓ cup butter, melted

2 tablespoons all-purpose flour

2 teaspoons vanilla

2 teaspoons ground cinnamon, divided

¾ teaspoon ground nutmeg, divided

1 unbaked 9-inch pie crust

Whipped cream and additional ground cinnamon (optional)

1. Preheat oven to 350°F. Peel and core apples; cut into small pieces. Place apples in medium bowl; cover with cold water and set aside.

2. Beat eggs in medium bowl with electric mixer at low speed until blended. Add all but 1 teaspoon sugar, buttermilk, butter, flour, vanilla, 1 teaspoon cinnamon and ½ teaspoon nutmeg; beat until well blended.

3. Drain apples well; place in unbaked crust. Pour buttermilk mixture over apples. Combine remaining 1 teaspoon sugar, 1 teaspoon cinnamon and ¼ teaspoon nutmeg in small bowl; sprinkle over top.

4. Bake 50 to 60 minutes or until knife inserted into center comes out clean. Serve warm or at room temperature. Top with whipped cream and additional cinnamon, if desired.

PRALINE PUMPKIN TART

MAKES 8 SERVINGS

1¼ cups all-purpose flour

1 tablespoon granulated sugar

¾ teaspoon salt, divided

¼ cup cold shortening, cut into small pieces

¼ cup (½ stick) cold butter, cut into small pieces

3 to 4 tablespoons cold water

1 can (15 ounces) solid-pack pumpkin

1 can (12 ounces) evaporated milk

⅔ cup packed brown sugar

2 eggs

1 teaspoon ground cinnamon

½ teaspoon ground ginger

¼ teaspoon ground cloves

Praline Topping (recipe follows)

1. Combine flour, granulated sugar and ¼ teaspoon salt in large bowl; mix well. Cut in shortening and butter with pastry blender or two knives until coarse crumbs form. Sprinkle with water, 1 tablespoon at a time, stirring with fork until dough holds together. Shape dough into a ball; wrap with plastic wrap. Refrigerate about 1 hour or until chilled.

2. Roll out dough into 13×9-inch rectangle on lightly floured surface. Press dough into bottom and up sides of 11×7-inch baking dish. Cover with plastic wrap; refrigerate 30 minutes.

3. Preheat oven to 400°F. Pierce crust with tines of fork at ¼-inch intervals. Line baking dish with foil; fill with dried beans, uncooked rice or ceramic pie weights.

4. Bake 10 minutes or until crust is set. Gently remove foil lining and beans; bake 5 minutes or until golden brown. Cool completely on wire rack.

5. Beat pumpkin, evaporated milk, brown sugar, eggs, cinnamon, remaining ½ teaspoon salt, ginger and cloves in large bowl with electric mixer at low speed until well blended. Pour into prepared crust. Bake 35 minutes.

6. Meanwhile, prepare Praline Topping. Sprinkle topping over tart. Bake 15 minutes or until knife inserted 1 inch from center comes out clean. Cool completely on wire rack.

PRALINE TOPPING: Combine ⅓ cup packed brown sugar, ⅓ cup chopped pecans and ⅓ cup quick oats in small bowl; mix well. Cut in 1 tablespoon softened butter with pastry blender or two knives until coarse crumbs form.

SWEET POTATO HONEY PIE

MAKES 8 SERVINGS

1 refrigerated pie crust
  (half of 15-ounce
  package)

1 can (29 ounces) cut-up
  sweet potatoes

2 eggs

⅔ cup honey

2 tablespoons butter,
  melted

¾ teaspoon ground
  cinnamon

½ teaspoon salt

½ teaspoon ground ginger

¼ teaspoon ground cloves

1 cup whole milk

  Whipped cream and
  ground nutmeg
  (optional)

1. Preheat oven to 425°F. Line 9-inch pie plate with crust; flute edge.

2. Drain sweet potatoes, reserving 2 tablespoons liquid. Place sweet potatoes and liquid in food processor; pulse until smooth. Measure 2½ cups, reserving any remaining purée for another use.

3. Whisk eggs in large bowl. Add sweet potato purée, honey, butter, cinnamon, salt, ginger and cloves; whisk until well blended. Whisk in milk until blended. Pour into crust.

4. Bake 15 minutes. *Reduce oven temperature to 350°F.* Bake 40 to 45 minutes or until filling is puffy. Cool on wire rack. Serve at room temperature or chilled; top with whipped cream and nutmeg, if desired.

DESSERTS

GINGER PEAR COBBLER

MAKES 8 TO IO SERVINGS

7 firm ripe d'Anjou pears (about 3½ pounds), peeled and cut into ½-inch pieces

⅓ cup packed brown sugar

1 cup plus 2 tablespoons all-purpose flour, divided

2 tablespoons lemon juice

2 teaspoons ground ginger, divided

½ teaspoon ground cinnamon

⅛ teaspoon ground nutmeg

¼ cup plus 1 tablespoon granulated sugar, divided

1½ teaspoons baking powder

¼ teaspoon salt

¼ cup (½ stick) butter, cut into small pieces

¼ cup whipping cream

1 egg, lightly beaten

1. Preheat oven to 375°F. Spray 9-inch square baking dish with nonstick cooking spray.

2. Combine pears, brown sugar, 2 tablespoons flour, lemon juice, 1 teaspoon ginger, cinnamon and nutmeg in large bowl; toss to coat. Spoon into prepared baking dish.

3. Combine remaining 1 cup flour, 1 teaspoon ginger, ¼ cup granulated sugar, baking powder and salt in medium bowl. Add butter; mix with fingertips until shaggy clumps form. Add cream and egg; stir just until combined. Drop topping, 2 tablespoons at a time, into mounds over pear mixture. Sprinkle with remaining 1 tablespoon granulated sugar.*

4. Bake 40 to 45 minutes or until filling is bubbly and topping is golden brown.

Or substitute 1 tablespoon coarse sugar to sprinkle over top of cobbler.

PUMPKIN BREAD PUDDING

MAKES 2 SERVINGS

2 slices whole wheat bread

1 cup solid-pack pumpkin

1 egg

2 tablespoons sugar

1 teaspoon vanilla

½ teaspoon ground cinnamon

1 tablespoon raisins

Whipped cream (optional)

1. Preheat oven to 375°F. Spray 2 ovenproof bowls or custard cups with nonstick cooking spray.

2. Toast bread; cut into 1-inch cubes.

3. Whisk pumpkin, egg, sugar, vanilla and cinnamon in medium bowl until well blended. Gently fold in toast cubes and raisins until blended. Divide mixture evenly between prepared bowls.

4. Bake 30 minutes. Serve warm with whipped cream, if desired.

APPLE CRANBERRY CRUMBLE

MAKES 4 SERVINGS

4 large apples (about 1⅓ pounds), peeled and cut into ¼-inch slices

2 cups fresh or frozen cranberries

⅓ cup granulated sugar

6 tablespoons all-purpose flour, divided

1 teaspoon apple pie spice, divided

¼ teaspoon salt, divided

½ cup chopped walnuts

¼ cup old-fashioned oats

2 tablespoons packed brown sugar

¼ cup (½ stick) butter, cut into small pieces

1. Preheat oven to 375°F.

2. Combine apples, cranberries, granulated sugar, 2 tablespoons flour, ½ teaspoon apple pie spice and ⅛ teaspoon salt in large bowl; toss to coat. Spoon into medium cast iron skillet.

3. Combine remaining 4 tablespoons flour, walnuts, oats, brown sugar, remaining ½ teaspoon apple pie spice and ⅛ teaspoon salt in medium bowl; mix well. Cut in butter with pastry blender or two knives until mixture resembles coarse crumbs. Sprinkle over fruit mixture in skillet.

4. Bake 50 to 60 minutes or until filling is bubbly and topping is lightly browned.

BANANAS FOSTER CRISP

MAKES 8 TO 10 SERVINGS

¾ cup packed dark brown sugar, divided

6 tablespoons (¾ stick) butter, divided

3 tablespoons dark rum

½ teaspoon ground cinnamon

¼ teaspoon grated nutmeg

8 medium bananas (firm, yellow, no spots), cut into ½-inch slices (about 6 cups)

½ cup all-purpose flour

½ cup chopped pecans

¼ teaspoon salt

Vanilla ice cream (optional)

1. Place oven rack in lower-middle position. Preheat oven to 375°F. Spray 8-inch round or square baking dish with nonstick cooking spray.

2. Combine ½ cup brown sugar and 2 tablespoons butter in small saucepan; cook and stir over medium heat about 3 minutes or until butter has melted and sugar has dissolved. Slowly add rum, cinnamon and nutmeg (mixture will spatter); cook 1 minute, stirring constantly. Pour mixture into large bowl. Add bananas; toss to coat. Spoon into prepared baking dish.

3. Combine flour, pecans, remaining ¼ cup brown sugar and salt in medium bowl; mix well. Cut remaining 4 tablespoons butter into small pieces. Add to flour mixture; mix with fingertips until mixture forms coarse crumbs. Sprinkle over banana mixture.

4. Bake 40 minutes or until filling is bubbly and topping is golden brown. Let stand 1 hour before serving. Serve with ice cream, if desired.

PUMPKIN CRÈME BRÛLÉE

MAKES 4 SERVINGS

1 cup whipping cream

1 cup half-and-half

½ cup granulated sugar

¼ teaspoon salt

¼ teaspoon ground cinnamon

Pinch ground nutmeg (optional)

4 egg yolks

½ cup solid-pack pumpkin

4 tablespoons packed brown sugar

1. Preheat oven to 300°F. Spray 4 (1-cup) shallow ramekins or custard cups with nonstick cooking spray.

2. Combine cream, half-and-half, granulated sugar, salt, cinnamon and nutmeg, if desired, in medium saucepan; bring to a simmer over medium-high heat.

3. Beat egg yolks in heatproof bowl. Gradually whisk in one fourth of hot cream mixture. Slowly pour egg yolk mixture back into remaining cream mixture in saucepan, whisking constantly until slightly thickened. Remove from heat; whisk in pumpkin until well blended. Pour into prepared ramekins.

4. Place ramekins in 9-inch square baking pan; place in oven. Pour hot water into baking pan to depth of 1 inch.

5. Bake 45 to 55 minutes or until set. Cool in pan 30 minutes. Remove ramekins from pan; refrigerate at least 1 hour.

6. Preheat broiler. Sprinkle 1 tablespoon brown sugar evenly over each custard. Place ramekins on baking sheet. Broil 4 inches from heat 1 minute or until sugar begins to bubble and turns golden brown. Cool 15 minutes before serving.

BAKED APPLE CUSTARD

MAKES 6 SERVINGS

1½ cups unsweetened
    applesauce

1 teaspoon ground
    cinnamon

¼ teaspoon salt

4 eggs

½ cup half-and-half

¼ cup unsweetened apple
    juice concentrate

½ teaspoon ground nutmeg

1. Preheat oven to 350°F.

2. Combine applesauce, cinnamon and salt in large bowl; mix well. Add eggs, half-and-half and apple juice concentrate; whisk until well blended. Pour into shallow 1½-quart or 8-inch square baking dish.

3. Place baking dish in shallow roasting pan. Pour hot water into roasting pan to reach 1 inch up sides of baking dish. Sprinkle custard with nutmeg.

4. Bake 45 minutes or until knife inserted near center of custard comes out clean. Cool completely on wire rack. Cover and refrigerate 1 hour or overnight.

TANGY CRANBERRY COBBLER

MAKES 6 SERVINGS

2 cups fresh or thawed frozen cranberries

1 cup dried cranberries

1 cup raisins

½ cup orange juice

¼ cup plus 2 tablespoons sugar, divided

2 teaspoons cornstarch

1 cup all-purpose flour

2 teaspoons baking powder

1 teaspoon ground cinnamon

¼ teaspoon salt

¼ cup (½ stick) cold butter, cut into small pieces

½ cup milk

1. Preheat oven to 400°F.

2. Combine fresh cranberries, dried cranberries, raisins, orange juice, ¼ cup sugar and cornstarch in 9-inch square baking dish; toss to coat.

3. Combine flour, remaining 2 tablespoons sugar, baking powder, cinnamon and salt in large bowl; mix well. Cut in butter with pastry blender or two knives until mixture resembles coarse crumbs. Add milk; stir just until moistened. Drop batter by large spoonfuls over cranberry mixture.

4. Bake 35 to 40 minutes or until topping is golden brown. Serve warm.

PANETTONE BREAD PUDDING

MAKES 12 SERVINGS

½ (2-pound) loaf panettone bread, cut into ¾-inch cubes (8 cups)

6 eggs

½ cup sugar

3 cups half-and-half

1 teaspoon vanilla

½ teaspoon ground cinnamon

¼ teaspoon salt

Powdered sugar

Caramel ice cream topping

1. Preheat oven to 350°F. Spray 11×7-inch baking dish with nonstick cooking spray.

2. Spread bread cubes in prepared baking dish. Whisk eggs and sugar in large bowl until blended. Add half-and-half, vanilla, cinnamon and salt; whisk until well blended. Pour over bread, pressing down to moisten top. Let stand 15 minutes.

3. Bake 40 to 45 minutes or until puffed and golden brown. Serve warm or at room temperature.

4. Sprinkle with powdered sugar; drizzle with caramel topping.

INDIVIDUAL CHOCOLATE SOUFFLÉS

MAKES 2 SOUFFLÉS

1 tablespoon butter, plus additional for greasing

2 tablespoons plus 1 teaspoon sugar, divided

4 ounces bittersweet chocolate, broken into pieces

2 eggs, separated, at room temperature

Powdered sugar (optional)

1. Preheat oven to 375°F. Grease 2 (¾-cup) soufflé dishes or ramekins with butter. Add ½ teaspoon sugar to each dish; shake to coat bottoms and sides.

2. Combine chocolate and 1 tablespoon butter in top of double boiler; heat over simmering water until chocolate is melted and smooth, stirring occationally. Remove from heat; stir in egg yolks, one at a time, until blended. (Mixture may become grainy, but will smooth out with addition of egg whites.)

3. Beat egg whites in medium bowl with electric mixer at high speed until soft peaks form. Gradually add remaining 2 tablespoons sugar; beat until stiff peaks form and mixture is glossy.

4. Gently fold egg whites into chocolate mixture. Do not overmix; allow some white streaks to remain. Divide batter evenly between prepared dishes.

5. Bake 15 minutes until soufflés rise but remain moist in centers. Serve immediately; sprinkle with powdered sugar, if desired.

CRANBERRY APPLE CRISP

1 cup old-fashioned oats

¾ cup all-purpose flour

½ cup packed brown sugar

2 teaspoons finely chopped crystallized ginger

½ teaspoon ground cinnamon

¼ teaspoon salt

6 tablespoons (¾ stick) butter, cut into small pieces

1 can (16 ounces) whole berry cranberry sauce

2 tablespoons cornstarch

5 cups peeled and thinly sliced apples (about 5 medium)

Whipped cream or ice cream (optional)

1. Preheat oven to 375°F.

2. Combine oats, flour, brown sugar, crystallized ginger, cinnamon and salt in medium bowl; mix well. Cut in butter with pastry blender or two knives until mixture resembles coarse crumbs.

3. Combine cranberry sauce and cornstarch in large saucepan; heat over medium-high heat 2 minutes or until sauce bubbles, stirring occasionally. Add apples; toss to coat. Spoon into 8-inch square baking dish; sprinkle with oat mixture.

4. Bake 25 to 35 minutes or until apples are tender and topping is golden brown. Serve warm with whipped cream, if desired.

GINGERED PUMPKIN CUSTARD

MAKES 6 SERVINGS

¾ cup sugar

2 eggs

1½ teaspoons ground cinnamon

½ teaspoon salt

½ teaspoon ground nutmeg

1 can (15 ounces) solid-pack pumpkin

1¼ cups half-and-half

3 tablespoons finely chopped candied ginger, divided

Whipped cream (optional)

1. Preheat oven to 375°F. Place 6 (8-ounce) ramekins or custard cups on baking sheet.

2. Whisk sugar, eggs, cinnamon, salt and nutmeg in medium bowl until blended. Add pumpkin and half-and-half; whisk until well blended. Stir in 2 tablespoons ginger. Pour into ramekins.

3. Bake 35 to 40 minutes or until knife inserted into centers comes out clean. Cool on wire rack at least 20 minutes before serving.

4. Serve warm or at room temperature with whipped cream, if desired. Sprinkle with remaining 1 tablespoon ginger.

VARIATION: To make one large dish of custard instead of individual servings, pour the custard mixture into a greased 8-inch or 1½-quart baking dish. Bake 45 minutes or until a knife inserted into the center comes out clean.

APPLE PIE POCKETS

MAKES 4 SERVINGS

2 pieces lavash bread,
   each cut into
   4 rectangles

2 tablespoons melted
   butter

¾ cup apple pie filling

1 egg, beaten with
   1 teaspoon water

½ cup powdered sugar

⅛ teaspoon ground
   cinnamon

2½ teaspoons milk

1. Preheat oven to 400°F. Line baking sheet with parchment paper.

2. Brush one side of each lavash piece with butter. Place half of pieces, buttered side down, on work surface. Spoon 3 tablespoons pie filling in center of each piece, leaving ½-inch border. Brush border with egg mixture. Top with remaining lavash pieces, buttered side up. Press edges together with fork to seal. Cut 3 small slits in center of each pie with paring knife. Place on prepared baking sheet.

3. Bake 18 minutes or until crust is crisp and golden brown. Remove to wire rack to cool 15 minutes.

4. Combine powdered sugar, cinnamon and milk in small bowl; whisk until smooth. Drizzle over pies; let stand 15 minutes to allow glaze to set slightly.

METRIC CONVERSION CHART

VOLUME MEASUREMENTS (dry)

$1/8$ teaspoon = 0.5 mL
$1/4$ teaspoon = 1 mL
$1/2$ teaspoon = 2 mL
$3/4$ teaspoon = 4 mL
1 teaspoon = 5 mL
1 tablespoon = 15 mL
2 tablespoons = 30 mL
$1/4$ cup = 60 mL
$1/3$ cup = 75 mL
$1/2$ cup = 125 mL
$2/3$ cup = 150 mL
$3/4$ cup = 175 mL
1 cup = 250 mL
2 cups = 1 pint = 500 mL
3 cups = 750 mL
4 cups = 1 quart = 1 L

VOLUME MEASUREMENTS (fluid)

1 fluid ounce (2 tablespoons) = 30 mL
4 fluid ounces ($1/2$ cup) = 125 mL
8 fluid ounces (1 cup) = 250 mL
12 fluid ounces ($1 1/2$ cups) = 375 mL
16 fluid ounces (2 cups) = 500 mL

WEIGHTS (mass)

$1/2$ ounce = 15 g
1 ounce = 30 g
3 ounces = 90 g
4 ounces = 120 g
8 ounces = 225 g
10 ounces = 285 g
12 ounces = 360 g
16 ounces = 1 pound = 450 g

DIMENSIONS

$1/16$ inch = 2 mm
$1/8$ inch = 3 mm
$1/4$ inch = 6 mm
$1/2$ inch = 1.5 cm
$3/4$ inch = 2 cm
1 inch = 2.5 cm

OVEN TEMPERATURES

250°F = 120°C
275°F = 140°C
300°F = 150°C
325°F = 160°C
350°F = 180°C
375°F = 190°C
400°F = 200°C
425°F = 220°C
450°F = 230°C

BAKING PAN SIZES

Utensil	Size in Inches/Quarts	Metric Volume	Size in Centimeters
Baking or Cake Pan (square or rectangular)	8×8×2	2 L	20×20×5
	9×9×2	2.5 L	23×23×5
	12×8×2	3 L	30×20×5
	13×9×2	3.5 L	33×23×5
Loaf Pan	8×4×3	1.5 L	20×10×7
	9×5×3	2 L	23×13×7
Round Layer Cake Pan	8×1½	1.2 L	20×4
	9×1½	1.5 L	23×4
Pie Plate	8×1¼	750 mL	20×3
	9×1¼	1 L	23×3
Baking Dish or Casserole	1 quart	1 L	—
	1½ quart	1.5 L	—
	2 quart	2 L	—